ECHOES FROM HEAVEN

By

FLORA B. FOSTER

First Fruits Press
Wilmore, Kentucky
c2016

Echoes from Heaven. By Flora B. Foster

First Fruits Press, ©2016

Previously published by the Pentecostal Publishing Company, ©1913.

ISBN: 9781621715283 (print) 9781621715290 (digital) 9781621715306 (kindle)

Digital version at http://place.asburyseminary.edu/firstfruitsheritagematerial/126/

Foster, Flora B.

Echoes from Heaven / by Flora B. Foster. Wilmore, Kentucky : First Fruits Press, ©2016.

127 pages : illustrations, portraits ; 21 cm.

Poems.

Reprint. Previously published: Louisville, Kentucky : Pentecostal Publishing Company, ©1913.

ISBN - 13: 9781621715283

1. Christian poetry, American. I. Title.

PS3511.O688 E4 2016

Cover design by Jonathan Ramsay

asburyseminary.edu
800.2ASBURY
204 North Lexington Avenue
Wilmore, Kentucky 40390

First Fruits
THE ACADEMIC OPEN PRESS OF ASBURY SEMINARY

First Fruits Press
The Academic Open Press of Asbury Theological Seminary
204 N. Lexington Ave., Wilmore, KY 40390
859-858-2236
first.fruits@asburyseminary.edu
asbury.to/firstfruits

Flora B. Foster.

Echoes From Heaven.

By

Flora B. Foster.

The words were spoken in heaven,
Their echoes came to earth,
We caught them ere they scattered,
'Twas thus our book had birth.

He that hath my word, let him speak my word faithfully.—Jer. 23:28.

Pentecostal Publishing Company, Publishers.
Louisville, Ky.

CONTENTS.

4 *Contents*

INTRODUCTION.

The author of this little volume of verse is well known to the writer of these introductory words as a most devoted and earnest Christian. While laboring under certain limitations due to physical infirmity, she abounds with zeal for the accomplishment of such service as shall glorify the Redeemer of men in helping to advance His kingdom in the earth. She lives to serve her Lord in helpful service to the children of men. This is the motive which has led her to attempt this unpretentious little volume of what may be termed Sermons in Rhyme. There is some portion in its contents for people of almost every class; and none who read can fail to perceive that these productions breathe a fervent Christian spirit, the chief aim of which is to benefit the reader. While making no claim to anything like literary perfection, she does indulge the hope that her readers may be sympathetic with her purpose, and that each one may find something in the verses she has penned that will be inspiring and helpful.   Another object the author has had in the writing of this volume is that of procuring something through its circulation with which to do good in the world.   She delights in helping every good cause, and has but little except what she can earn with her pen for this purpose.   Therefore those who purchase and help to circulate "Echoes from Heaven" will be helping her to realize this object of her heart's desire, in addition to the personal benefit they may receive from what she has written.   I certainly hope the circulation of the book and the good accomplished thereby may far exceed her highest anticipations.   WILSON T. HOGUE.

Michigan City, Indiana.

Rev. A. Foster.

DEDICATION.

To My Father, Rev. A. Foster.

In fond mem'ry I can see you
    As you used to sit and write,
Silent was your meditation
    Long into the hours of night.

I remember once your saying,
    As you gave a loving look,
"'Tis a thought I long have cherished,
    Belle, I wish you'd write a book."

Those few words to me you whispered
    Were engraved upon my heart,
'Twas the thought that day you uttered,
    That caused me this book to start.

Others thought I could not do it,
    Said, "You never will succeed:"
So I did not ask their counsel,
    To their words I gave no heed.

7

As I looked above for guidance,
　Such an inspiration fell
That my inmost thoughts and feelings
　I could never, never tell.

And though now you are in Heaven,
　On this page you ne'er can look
Yet to you my sainted father,
　I now dedicate this book.

As 'tis sent forth on its mission
　I trust many hearts will glow,
Souls be fed, and hope made brighter,
　And that faith will stronger grow.

And when I am called to enter
　Into my inheritance,
All the good this work's accomplished,
　We will see on backward glance.

Every man's work shall be made manifest.—1
Cor. 3:13.

And behold I come quickly; and my reward is
with me to give every man according as his work
shall be.—Rev. 21:12.

Sarah C. Foster.

TO MY MOTHER.

Long and weary is the journey
    Of your pilgrimage below.
Fourscore years and five, my mother,
    You've seen seasons come and go.

Summer's suns have beamed upon you,
    Winter's snows have fallen fast.
But you're nearing now the gateway
    Where all earthly things are past.

Though so faithfully you've labored,
    Still your work is not quite done;
You must toil a little longer
    Ere the guerdon you have won.

Yes, we need you here to cheer us,
    Need your counsel, need your prayer,
We thank God each morn that breaketh
    That he yet your life doth spare.

Soon you've gone to be with father,
    Brother John, sweet Carrie too,
And the babes, torn from your bosom
    Will again be pressed to you.

Many friends up there will greet you,
  Loving hands will clasp your own,
Many souls be thrilled with rapture,
  While we here will weep alone.

But those days will not be lengthened
  Soon the blessed Lord will come
When his Bride will rise to meet him,
  And the Saints be gathered home.

O, 'twill be a joyous meeting—
  That reunion in the sky.
Here we weep, but there "The Father"
  Wipes the tears from every eye.

And God shall wipe away all tears from their
eyes; and there shall be no more death. neither sor-
row, nor crying. neither shall there be any more
pain, for the former things are passed away.—
Rev. 21 :4.

Part One.

Pertaining to God and Heaven.

And there came a voice from Heaven, saying, "Thou art my beloved son in whom I am well pleased."—Mark 1:11.

Behold the Lamb of God which taketh away the sin of the world.—Jno. 1:29.

And he carried me away in the spirit to a great and high mountain, and showed me that great city, the holy Jerusalem. . . . And there shall in no wise enter into it anything that defileth. . . But they which are written in the Lamb's book of life—Rev. 21:10-27.

WHERE IS HEAVEN?

O mother, is Heaven some far off place,
   Way up above the sky,
Where none can see the Savior's face,
   Nor to his side draw nigh?

No, dear one, Heaven is not so far—
   Sometimes 'tis very near;
We have a foretaste where we are
   In ev'ry smile and tear.

We find it in each flower that blooms
   In ev'ry shrub and tree,
And in the words of him who said,
   "Let children come to me."

We find it in the rolling tide
   And in the rippling stream;
We find it in the fields so wide,
   And in the pastures green.

'Tis Heaven to help the weak ones on,
  To dry the falling tear.
'Tis Heaven to lead one soul to God
  Or speak one word of cheer.

And if eternity we'd spend
  In Heaven with Christ the Lord,
We must while here abide in him,
  Must listen to his word.

In my Father's house are many mansions, if it
were not so I would have told you: I go to prepare
a place for you, and if I go and prepare a place for
you, I will come again and receive you unto myself,
that where I am, there ye may be also.—Jno.
14 :1-3.

LOOKING UPWARD.

I will lift up mine eyes unto the hills from whence cometh my help;

My help cometh from the Lord which made heaven and earth.—Psa. 121:1, 2.

The great One who is lofty and holy
    Is watching us now from on high;
And He says that He'll draw very near us
    If now unto Him we draw nigh.

And so always, if we're looking upward,
    We hear such sweet words from above;
And O, then, as He draws us still closer
    We learn of His wonderful love.

We learn more than to know how He loves us
    We learn what He'd have us to do.
In affliction we hear His voice saying,
    "I send what will prove best for you."

Let us all then confidingly trust Him,
    Nor doubt where we can't understand;
Ever keeping our eyes on the Master
    While marching toward heaven's fair land.

ENTRANCE TO HEAVEN.

For so an entrance shall be granted unto you abundantly, into the everlasting Kingdom of our Lord and Savior Jesus Christ.—2 Peter 1:11.

Do you wish to enter heaven
    Empty handed and alone,
When you might go in rejoicing,
    Bearing sheaves up to the throne?

Do you wish to enter heaven
    As one would from fire escape,
When you might go in triumphant,
    Sweeping through the pearly gate?

Do you wish to wear forever
    A dull crown without a star,
When you might be always shining
    Bright as now the heavens are?

Do you know that up in heaven
    There awaits a great reward,
For the souls that here are working
    Heartily as to the Lord?

Let us then arouse to action,
   Let us stir the gift within,
And go bravely to the battle,
   Fighting 'gainst the hosts of sin.

No, we must not be discouraged,
   Though Sin's battlements are high,
Though his armies fall upon us
   Like a cyclone from the sky.

When the Son of Man returneth,
   Shall there faith on earth be found?
Or will He find us disheartened,
   Looking downward to the ground?

What though sinners will not listen
   To the words we have to say,
When we plead, "Come unto Jesus."
   They will scoff and turn away;

God may use the words we've spoken
   To convert a wicked heart,
And he may return repentant,
   Seeking yet the better part.

THE BIRTH OF CHRIST.

And all they that heard, wondered at those things
which were told them by the shepherds.—Luke
2:18.

When Christ was born in Bethlehem
    And in the manger laid,
The shepherds sa wHis glory shine,
    And they were sore afraid.

As they were watching faithfully
    Their helpless flocks by night,
They looke and lo, the skies above
    Shone with a brilliant light.

They saw an angel of the Lord
    Who said "Be not afraid,
For Christ is born on earth this day
    And in a manger laid:

And I have come to bring to you
    Good tidings of great joy,
And peace to all His people that
    The world cannot destroy."

A multitude of angels bright
  Sang praise unto the name
Of Him who had the power given
  To break the prisoner's chain.

Then chanted all the Heavenly host,
  "To God all glory be
And all ye sons of men on earth
  Good will and peace to thee."

The vision and the angels voice
  Were gone, the earth was still,
The sheep were left alone to graze
  Upon the grassy hill.

The shepherds went to Bethlehem
  To see this wondrous sight,
And in a humble manger found
  The blessed Lord of light.

They spread the tidings far and wide,
  Told what they'd seen and heard,
And all that heard it were amazed
  And wondered at their word.

The shepherds praised the God of Heaven
  Who gave to them their part,—
But all these things the mother kept
  And pondered in her heart.

THE STORY OF JESUS.

Friends, we've come to speak of Jesus,
　　He's the one who saves from sin;
Won't you listen to the story,
　　Hear us while we talk of Him?
He hath laid the earth's foundation,
　　'Twas by Him all things were made,
He hath bought us and redeemed us,—
　　With His blood the price was paid.

Jesus, from His home in heaven,
　　Saw us in such deep distress,
For the curse of sin had entered
　　And He felt our helplessness.
Saw by nature man was sinful,
　　When he drew his infant breath,
For through sin he'd lost God's image,
　　And the penalty was death.

He saw there was none to rescue,
　　Saw that all were doomed to hell;
So He said, "I'll die to save them;"
　　Such love mortals can not tell.

Loved us so while we were sinners,
  That He left His home on high,
Came to earth and lived and suffered,
  Came for sinful man to die.

He was stricken, He was smitten,
  He was wounded, bruis'd sore,
There are none who here have suffered,
  But our Lord hath suffered more.
Though oppressed and sore afflicted,
  No complaint was ever heard,
As a lamb brought to the slaughter,
  Still He uttered not a word.

Yes, He died for your transgressions,
  'Twas for you He suffered all,
To restore to you his image,—
  To redeem you from the fall.
He can save you, He can keep you,
  Guide you all the journey through.
In temptation He can help you,
  For our Lord was tempted too.

Come to Jesus, let Him save you:
  Methinks you are wondering, "How,
When He died on Calvary's mountain,
  Can this Jesus save me now?"

Listen, while we try to tell you:—
From the tomb He rose again
And ascended up to Heaven
There to plead for sons of men.

When one prays to God the Father,
Asking pardon for his sin,
Jesus pleads, "O, Father, save him,
For my blood was shed for him."
Jesus' blood for sin's remission,
Let there be no other plea;
Come, then, pleading, "I'm a sinner,
Jesus' blood was shed for me."

Faith in Jesus' blood will save you,
We have proved the promise true;
From all sin His blood doth cleanse us,
It will do the same for you.
If you leave your sinful wanderings
And repent and seek His grace.
When He comes we shall be like Him,
We shall see Him face to face.

Although now we cannot see Him,
Cannot see His face so meek,
Yet believing, we're rejoicing
With a joy we may not speak,

Though we long to tell the story,
  Long to tell it now to you;
For it is so full of glory—
  And so full of rapture too.

But if we should talk forever,
  Still the half could not be told;
How He pardons and redeems us
  And then purifies like gold.
How He blesses, keeps and guides us,
  And so plain He makes His will,
While in every storm He whispers,
  "I am with thee; peace, be still!"

Friends, if you will seek this Jesus,
  If you search with all your heart,
He will pardon your transgressions,
  He'll show you the better part.
Show you how to live for Heaven,
  For He'd wash away your sin;
Fill you with His Holy Spirit,
  Give you perfect peace within.

For it was for you He suffered,
  'Twas for you He bled and died;

Why not come and seek salvation?
　　Come, you shall not be denied.
He'll forgive you, He'll receive you,
　　He will never cast away;
And the dreary night of darkness
　　Shall be changed to endless day.

Him that cometh to me, I will in no wise cast
out.—Jno. 6 :37.

CHRISTMAS GREETING.

Accept this token of our love,
    'Tis sent in mem'ry of the day
When Jesus Christ was born on earth
    Your sins and mine to take away.

He died for us that we might live
    A life that's hid with Christ in God,—
In perfect love and joy and peace,
    By simply trusting in His word.

Each precious promise we may claim
    If we each solemn warning heed;
Let's daily cast on Him our care
    For He'll supply our ev'ry need.

Let's follow closely in His steps;
    As He walked, humbly, so should we;
And He said, "What ye've done to these
    Of mine ye've likewise done to me."

LET THE SAVIOR IN.

Are you weak and heavy laden,
   Burdened with a load of sin?
Jesus at the door is knocking;
   Open now and let Him in.

Jesus Christ the world's redeemer
   Shed His precious blood for thee:
Hear His pleading voice now calling
   "Come ye, come ye unto me."

Yes, the gentle, loving Jesus
   Stands with open arms for you;
He is waiting to receive you,
   He will take you safely through.

Won't you ope' the door for Jesus?
   Won't you let the Savior in?
He'll forgive all your transgressions,
   He will cleanse your heart from sin.

CHORUS.

Open now, open wide,
   Let the precious Savior in,
He'll forgive, He'll receive,
   He will make you free from sin.

THE STORY OF THE WISE MEN.

Now when Jesus was born in the land of Judea,
  Behold there came men from a land very far:
"Where is he that is born as an heir to the king-
    dom?"
  They asked of the king, "We have seen his bright
    star."

Then the jealous King Herod, was troubled and
    fearful,
  Lest he from his kingly robes soon should be
    shorn,
So he gathered the chief priests and scribes all
    together,
  Demanding of them, where the Christ should be
    born.

And they told him, "In Bethlehem, land of Judea,
  A Governor, ruling the people of God,
Shall come forth from a root as a lively branch
    springing,
  We find it thus written in God's holy word."

Then the wise men were asked when they first saw
    the star;
  And were told to go search; then bring word to
      the king,
So that he too might share in the worship and
    praise,
  That as they gave their gifts, he his homage
      would bring.

Then the wise men departed, and lo, see the star!
  For it went on before till its bright light was cast
O'er the place where the child was, their Savior and
    king,
  And their joy was complete, they had found Him
    at last.

  They bowed down on their knees, and they wor-
    shipped him there:
And they poured out their gold, precious treasures of
    earth,
Then they gave Him their frankincense—worship
    and prayer:
  But the myrrh, or their love, was the greatest of
    worth.

They returned not to Herod, for God gave them
    warning:
  An angel was sent unto Joseph by night,
Saying, "Herod will seek the young child to de-
    stroy Him;
  Arise, take the child into Egypt by flight."

So the antitype, Christ, like the type in past ages,
  Out of Egypt was called by the great Holy One;
And thus were fulfilled the strange words of Je-
    hovah,
  Who said, "Out of Egypt I've called my own
    Son."

Herod slew all the children of Bethlehem then;
  Lamentation and mourning and weeping were
    there,
For each infant was torn from the breast of its
    mother:
  The king was so cruel, not one did he spare.

Part Two.

Prayer.

Whatsoever ye shall ask in prayer, believing ye shall receive. Matt. 21:22.

If ye abide in me and my words abide in you, ye shall ask what ye will and it shall be done.— Jno. 15:7.

And in the morning, rising up a great while before day, He went out and departed into a solitary place and there prayed.—Mark 1:35.

PRAYER.

Prayer is holding sweet communion with the Father
    and the Son,
When each word, each thought is prompted by the
    the blessed Holy One.
Prayer is looking up toward Heaven, prayer is talk-
    ing with the Lord,
Telling Him our heart's desire, listening to his pre-
    cious word.

When we are in perfect concord with the Father
    and the Son,
And can say, in deepest anguish, "Not my will but
    Thine be done;"
Then it is the clouds are rifted, and we hear a
    sweet voice say,
"Fear ye not, keep looking upward; lo, I'm with
    you all th way."

When our hearts do not condemn us, but assure us
    we are right,
And we keep all His commandments, do what's
    pleasing in His sight,

Then it is we claim the promise of the one beloved
    Son—
"Whatso'er ve ask the Father in my name it shall
    be done."

We kneel—all around is darkness; we arise—lo!
    all is light;
Kneeling in our utter weakness, rising, strengthened
    with His might.
Whence this peaceful love of heaven? Why this
    change within my breast?
Tried one, 'tis a loving Father hears his child and
    sends sweet rest.

'Tis the blessed yoke of Jesus, 'tis the holy Fath-
    er's will.
He says, though the storm is raging, "I am with
    with thee, peace be still."
He'll not leave us nor forsake us, He will never let
    us fall,
If we're watching, waiting, working, trusting Je-
    sus, this is all.

INTERCESSION.

And he saw that there was no man and wondered
that there was no intercession.—Ist. 59:16.

We have a message for you, friends,
    A message from the sky;
It came while kneeling down so low
    That Jesus heard our cry.

We asked Him why the harvest fields
    Which look so rich and ripe
Were not all garnered in the day,
    Why some were left till night?

Why grain though cut, was sometimes left
    In fields to rot and mould?
Why fruit was often left on trees
    Through winter's storm and cold?

We asked why men and women too
    Would not for mercy cry?
And why the poor and weakly ones
    Were left to faint and die?

We ask him why the preachers seemed
　　To lack the old-time power?
Why, blessings come down drop by drop—
　　We need an April shower?

He said, "I send out some to sow,
　　And some I send to reap;
I bid them nourish little lambs,
　　And gently lead the sheep.

"The messengers who use the sword
　　Do cut the ripe grain down ,
But it takes interceding prayer
　　To raise it from the ground.

"Though preachers sit in Moses' seat,
　　O'er all this sin-cursed land,
They have no more the prayers of saints,
　　None to uphold the hand.

"And this is why the harvest fails,
　　Why sinners will not yield,
And why so oft the grain though cut,
　　Lies wasting in the field."

"I'm looking now," He said, "for some
  To weep and intercede,
For some to lift up holy hands
  In faith and love to plead."

Let's kneel to God in earnest prayer
  He's just the same today!
And if we plead as Moses pled,
  He'll hear us when we pray.

If we have faith like Abraham,
  Each promise we may claim,
And God will grant whate'er we will,
  If asked in Jesus' name.

We see so many fail and fall,
  So many going down—
O, friends, let's help them back to God;
  'Twill be our joy and crown.

And I looked and there was none to help, and
I wondered that there was none to uphold.—Isa.
63:5.

PREVAILING PRAYER.

If you or I would gain the ear of God,
And if in prayer we ever would prevail,
Ourselves a living sacrifice we must
Present to God in humble faith and trust.
Our wills must be submerged in His divine;
On His great ocean we must launch our boat;
Must cut the shore lines, and "Be not afraid;"
Abide in Christ as branches in the vine,
And His word, richly, must abide in us;
Deny ourselves the things this world affords,
And live and walk by simple faith each day:
Like Jesus go alone with God and pray,
(And He continued there all night in prayer).
We must believe that God the Father is
And that He does reward the diligent
Who daily seek to know and do His will;
Then we must importune and plead with God,
And e'en at midnight, sometimes, rise and pray;
Like Jacob, wrestle until we prevail.
And though on us the en'my's darts are hurled,
Clad in God's armor we can firmly stand.
He'll always cause us to triumph through Christ,
And give us richly all things to enjoy,
And He will grant to us our heart's desire,
And we shall see the travail of our soul
And bring forth fruit to glorify His name.

A PRAYER FOR MY BIBLE CLASS.

O God, anoint my lips of clay
To speak thy word, I humbly pray;
That souls may see and understand,
And enter into Canaan's land.

The place where thou dost give the power,
Through Christ, to triumph every hour;
Entirely free from fear and dread,
And always by thy Spirit led.

They long for inward peace and rest,
They're praying to be fully blest,
To be upheld by Thine own hand—
They're looking toward this promised land.

Each one would be made pure within;
Made free, indeed, from inbred sin,
That they may walk by faith each day,
And in the Spirit boldly pray.

Let patience have her perfect work,
The peace of God rule in each heart:
That in the secret place so sweet.
Each one may dwell, in Christ complete.

Part Three.

Missionary Poems.

Ye shall receive power after that the Holy Ghost is come upon you and ye shall be witnesses unto me both in Jerusalem and in all Judea, and in Samaria, and unto the uttermost parts of the earth.—Acts 1:8.

Go ye, therefore and teach all nations baptizing them in the name of the Father, and of the Son, and of the Holy Ghost; teaching them to observe all things whatsoever I have commanded you; and, lo, I am with you alway, even to the end of the world.—Matt. 28:19, 20.

A CALL FOR WORKERS.

Go ye into all the world and preach the gospel
to every creature.—Mark 16:15.

Go, bring the world to Jesus,
  Go tell them of His love,
And how He died on Calvary,
  That they might live above.
Yes, tell them of His suffering,
  The story of the cross,
And that to do without Him
  Means everlasting loss.

Go, tell them how He saved you,
  And made you free from sin,
And how He feeds and guides you,
  And keeps you pure within.
Oh, tell them how He loves them,
  He's pleading every day;
And that He says to seekers,
  "I am the Truth, the Way."

43

Oh, tell them of salvation,
　The joy, the peace, the love,
And that He's now preparing
　For them a home above.
Oh, who will go and tell them?
　The time is fleeting fast;
Our days will soon be ended,
　The harvest soon be passed!

"Go ye and teach all nations,"
　Is what we heard One say,
It is the voice of Jesus,
　And shall we not obey?
"Repent and seek salvation;
　The message that I send,
And lo, I'm with you alway,
　Yes, even to the end."

Teach them the words of Jesus
　That he will hear their prayer.
And that he kindly bids them
　To cast on Him their care.
That He took sin and sorrow,
　Bore all upon the tree,
And that He pities wanderers,
　And whispers, "Come to me."

Teach them to pray to Jesus,
  Most earnestly to plead,
And that He ever liveth
  For us to intercede.
That He says to the weary,
  "Come unto me and rest,"
And all who come and trust Him
  Are fully saved and blessed.

Oh, bring the lost to Jesus!
  He calls and calls again.
"Bring them to me, oh, bring them,
  And shall He call in vain?
Both far and near He'd gather;
  Oh, listen, hear Him, do;
He's calling now for workers,
  Hush! is He calling you?

He calls you, yes, He calls you,
  And He would have you go
And bring to Him the lost ones,
  You can not answer "No."
He says He'll go before you,
  The path make smooth and straight;
Can you not go and leave all
  For your bless'd Savior's sake?

For He will come again,—
　A Bridegroom for His bride:
And if we're true and faithful,
　We shall not be denied.
But reign with Him forever,
　In that bright home above,
And sing the songs of Jesus
　And everlasting love.

Then let us go forth weeping,
　That we may come with joy,
And let us bear the precious seed,
　God's word, without alloy;
That we may come again soon,
　And bring great sheaves of grain,
For all we lose for Jesus,
　We'll find is richest gain.

Would you have abundant entrance?
　Abound in good works now.
If you would shine forever
　With stars upon your brow,
Improve each day you live here,
　The moments as they go,
In winning souls for Jesus,
　Because He loves them so.

Then you may come rejoicing,
　　And you will hear him say,
"Well done, thou faithful servant,
　　Where hast thou gleaned today?"
And in the holy rapture
　　With all the saints above,
We'll shout and sing forever
　　Songs of redeeming love.

He that goeth forth and weepeth, bearing precious seed shall, doubtless, come again with rejoicing bringing his sheaves with him.—Psa. 126:6.

The field is the world.—Matt. 13:38.

PRAY FOR LABORERS.

Then saith he to his disciples, the harvest truly
is plenteous, but the laborers are few; Pray ye
therefore the Lord of the harvest, that he send
forth laborers into his harvest.—Matt. 9:37, 38.

O, pray the Lord of harvest
 To send forth reapers true;
The harvest is so great, but
 The laborers are so few.
If you then hear Him calling
 For help far o'er the sea,
Oh, let Him hear you saying,
 "Lord, here am I, send me."

Don't fail to go in springtime,
 Don't fail to sow the seed,
To work in faith for Jesus,
 He will supply thy need.
Then wait with long, long patience
 For sunshine and for rain,
If He bids, go in harvest
 And garner ripening grain.

But if the Master calls thee
　　To toil in vales unknown,
And sends forth other reapers
　　In fields where you have sown,
Your hand place in the Father's
　　And gladly say, "I'll go,"
We'll all rejoice together
　　Though here we reap or sow.

Also I heard the voice of the Lord saying, "Whom shall I send, and who will go for us? Then said I, "Here am I, send me." And he said, "Go."—Isa. 6 :8, 9.

WORKING FOR JESUS.

Some must stand on walls of Zion,
  Some must watch the flocks by night,
Some must sow the seed in springtime,
  Others reap where fields are white.

Some are sent to sick and dying.
  Some to feed and clothe the poor.
Some to gently lead the children,
  Some afflictions to endure.

Some are called to preach the gospel,
  In a far off heathen land
Some to do His will by giving
  Working with a willing hand.

All are called to shine for Jesus
  Each may know and do His will,
Though he bid to field of action
  Or to patiently stand still.

Many, many souls are dying
  Without knowledge of the Lord
Shall we sit at ease in Zion
  Or shall we proclaim His word.

CHORUS.

Let us watch, let us pray,
  Let us do the work He's given.
Let us hope, let us trust,
  Till we gain our home in heaven.

Go work today in my vineyard.—Matt. 20:28.

There are differences of administrations but the same Lord.—1 Cor. 12:5.

Be thou faithful unto death, and I will give thee a crown of life.—Rev. 2:10.

THE MISSIONARY ARMY.

Tune and Chorus, "Battle Hymn of the Republic."

I have seen a mighty army
Loyal, brave, and very strong,
Strong in faith, and love, and spirit,
Strong in work, and prayer, and song;
'Tis the missionary army,
As they speed their way along:
　　"Our cause is marching on."

Yes, they go to preach the gospel
Over on the heathen shore,
Telling them the wondrous story
They have never heard before;
The Commander of this army
Is the Christ whom we adore:
　　"Our cause is marching on."

Come and join this glorious army
That has never known retreat;
Brave the frosts and snows of winter,
Brave the summer's sun and heat;
And we'll reach the souls in darkness
Showing them the mercy seat:
　　"Our cause is marching on."

See the ransomed heathen coming,
With their hearts made pure and white;
Lo, our ranks they are recruiting,
Helping us the foe to fight;
Then take courage Christian soldiers,
Work and pray with all your might:
    "Our cause is marching on."

We shall see the desert blossom,
See it bloom abundantly,
See the earth filled with God's glory,
As the waters fill the sea;
Then we'll all rejoice together,
And we'll shout the victory:
    "Our cause is marching on."

When the King of glory cometh,
And we meet him in the air,
Both the sower and the reaper,
The immortal bliss will share;
They shall enter in triumphant,
And a crown forever wear:
    "Our cause is marching on."

Part Four.

Memorial Poems.

And I heard a voice from Heaven saying unto me, "Write, 'Blessed are the dead which die in the Lord from henceforth, Yea saith the Spirit, that They may rest from their labors; and their works do follow them."—Rev. 14:13.

LINES ON THE DEATH OF A FRIEND.

IN MEMORY OF L. F. MILLER, 1908.

A child of God has been called home,
    Called to receive the prize;
And though we see him here no more,
    We'll meet beyond the skies.
So suddenly his summons came—
    So brief the time for prayer;
He finished writing, closed his desk,
    Then lay unconscious there.

He suffered here a few brief hours,
    Then left this world of sin;
And to the place prepared above,
    With joy was ushered in.
His work is ended, and he now
    Is reaping his reward;
For all the time he toiled on earth,
    He labored in the Lord.

Though often he was overworked,
    With many cares oppressed,

He never failed to render aid
    To those he found distressed.
He carried Jesus in his heart,
    'Twas Jesus in his life,
And in each battle 'gainst the foe,
    Fought bravely in the strife.

As father he was faithful, kind;
    As husband strong and true:
So gentle, loving and so wise,
    He knew just what to do.
He always fed the hungry ones,
    And also clothed the poor;
And none who came in need of aid,
    Went empty from his door.

He saw a little crippled one
    Who struggled through the land,
And often helped her onward,
    By kind and willing hand.
The Master, from his home on high,
    Saw each kind deed and smiled;
Then said, "Ye did it unto me,
    For she's my little child."

We'll look for him when we have gained
    That blissful, happy home;
We know we'll find him singing there;
    We'll find him near the throne.
Then let us faithfully toil on,
    And keep our eyes above,
Till we are summoned home,
    To sing of Christ's redeeming love.

Inasmuch as ye have done it unto one of the least of these. . . . ye have done it unto me.—Matt. 25:40.

For we must all appear before the judgment seat of Christ: that every one may receive the things done in his body, according to that which he hath done, whether it be good or bad.—2 Cor. 5:10.

A TRIBUTE OF MEMORY.

DEDICATED TO ISAAC KESLER.

1909.

Three brothers came to Danville,—
  'Twas about six years ago,
And laid foundation for a church,
  And then they watched it grow.
Their time and strength and money too
  They freely poured in there,
Their days were spent in busy toil,—
  Their nights in earnest prayer.

They bore the heavy burdens,
  They helped the weak ones on;
Encouraging each the other, said,
  "In Jesus Christ be strong."
They saw that many souls were saved;
  Some joined their little band;
The gospel in its fulness
  Was preached freely from the stand.

One day God said to brother Dan,
   The oldest of the three,
"Set now thy house in order,
   For soon I'll send for thee;"
He laid his armor down and said
   "Farewell" to his dear love,
And dressed in garb of righteousness
   Went to his God above.

A double portion of his love
   Fell on the other two,
And they, together, worked and prayed,
   With hearts so firm, so true.
But soon the reaper Death, passed by,
   And said to brother Sam,
"Your work is done, your sheaf is ripe,
   Come, hasten to the Lamb."

And brother Sam was ready,
   Though his friends are sore bereft,
And of the loyal brothers three,
   Now only one is left.
O brother Isaac tremble not,
   For we'll all stand by you,
We love the cause for which you stand,
   We love your God so true.

And God says, "I will strengthen thee,
  Uphold thee with my hand,
Till you're again united
  In that upper better land."
Toil on a little longer,
  You'll soon have run the race,
Soon your dear Lord will come from Heaven,
  You'll see Him face to face.

And these bereft companions,
  Who in widowhood are dressed,
Will each be clothed in robes of white
  In that fair land of rest.
And there will be no parting there,
  No sorrow, pain nor tears;
But blissful joy and perfect peace,
  Through everlasting years.

But where is now their heritage,
  Each child to them so dear?
Does each one know "The Bridegroom comes?"
  The end is drawing near?
Has each the wedding garment?
  Are you ready one and all?
If not, He still is pleading,
  Won't you heed his loving call?

We hope in that great morning,
  When the heavenly roll is read.
There will not one be missing,
  None numbered with the dead.
And in the glad reunion,
  When on that bright shore all meet,
That each will know the other,
  And stand in Him complete.

O brothers, sisters, listen now,
  We have a word for you,
For we're still left to toil below,
  And there's much work to do.
First here's our little church
  Entrusted to our hands,
And we can hear Christ saying,
  "Feed my sheep" and "Feed my lambs."

Then there are those around us,
  In our homes and near each heart,
Whom we must bring to Jesus
  For they'er groping in the dark.
And Jesus may require each one
  At your hand or at mine;
Let's bravely push the battle on,
  For there's so little time.

And now to us He's speaking,
　We hear His voice each day,
"Send My gospel to the heath'hen,"
　We should go, or give, or pray.
And let us so abide in Him,
　That when He shall appear,
In confidence and without shame,
　We'll meet our Lord so dear.

For we must all stand before the judgment seat
of Christ.—Rom. 12 :10.

A TRIBUTE TO THE MEMORY OF WILLIE DURHAM.

"There shall be no night there." Rev. 22 :5.

Willie Durham, how we miss him!
　How we loved his voice in song,
How we loved to hear him praying,
　For those whom he felt were wrong!

Although he was weak in body,
　And in mind a little child,
He was given without measure
　Jesus' spirit meek and mild.

He knew all about salvation,
　Knew how "Jesus is the way."
And if we would enter heaven
　We should come without delay.

How he felt the holy fire
　Going through him like a flame,
As the water in baptism
　Was poured on in Jesus' name.

Willie loved the words of Jesus;
　　How he'd quote them o'er and o'er!
He grew rich in grace and mercy,
　　Rich in Jesus' wondrous lore.

Then he prayed for erring brothers,
　　Prayed that they might see the way,
Prayed that Jesus Christ would enter
　　And their night be changed to day.

When news came of one's salvation,
　　Willie'd shout and praise the Lord,
Yes, he'd clap his hands with rapture,
　　Praising Jesus for His word.

When he'd see his mother weeping
　　When with care or sorrow pressed,
He would kneel in prayer toward heaven,
　　Pray and plead 'till she was blessed.

When in body she was suff'ring
　　He again would look to God,
Who, his simple faith would honor
　　And take off affliction's rod.

Willie leaned upon his father,
  Trusted in his love and care,
And when "father" was beside him
  He would venture anywhere.

Little Martha was his playmate
  And he taught her how to pray,
And they'd pray when he was suff'ring
  Till the pain would go away.

His last prayer was for his sister
  Who was living without God,
When he saw his strength was waning
  Said, "We'll leave her with the Lord."

O, the depth of God's great riches,
  Of His wisdom, grace and love,
How He calls the babes and suckling,
  Uses them to point above.

When the great men and the mighty
  Scoff and turn away from God,
He will choose the weak and foolish,
  Send them out to preach His word.

Willie preached the bless'd gospel,
  Yes, he preached and sang and prayed,
Till the holy angels gathered
  In the room where he was laid.

As they bore his spirit heav'nward
  Where 'tis said "there'll be no night,"
Heaven's gates, it seemed, were opened:
  Oh, it was a blessed sight.

Willie now is up in heaven,
  One among the blood-washed throng;
On his head a crown is shining
  As he sings redemption's song.

And thinkest thou this, A man . . . . that thou
shalt escape the judgment of God.—Rom. 2:3.

IN MEMORY OF REBECCA E. PERIGO.
1912.

Our mother, dear, has been called home,
   Called to receive the prize;
She's waiting for us now in bliss,
   We'll meet beyond the skies.
We miss her in the home each day,
   We miss her love and care;
We miss her counsel, wise and good,
   We miss her voice in prayer.

Her place is vacant in the church
   Where, all these many years,
She served and suffered, sang and prayed,
   'Mid sorrow, pain and tears.
Her work was always wrought in faith;
   She labored in God's love;
Was always patient in her hope
   Of seeing Him above.

She never was discouraged, though
   Ofttimes the way looked dim,
She always rested in her God,
   She waited long for Him.

All her delight was in the Lord,
　And He gave her heart's desire,
She saw her prayers all answered—
　Ere called to "Come up higher."

We crave a double portion of
　Her love and holy power,—
That, never weary, never faint,
　We may walk with God each hour.
She lives in those she won for God,
　Although from us she's gone,
She's resting from her labor,
　And her works do follow on.

And the ransomed of the Lord shall return and
come to Zion with songs, and everlasting joy upon
their heads; they shall obtain joy and gladness,
and sorrow and sighing shall flee away.—Isa. 35:10.

HELEN.

IN MEMORY OF HELEN BEAN, 1912.

Little Helen's up in Heaven
  Playing 'round the kingly throne;
How we loved our precious angel!
  Yet God chose her for his own.

Though we long to see our darling,
  Long to fold her to our breast,
Yet we would not call her backward
  For we're sure God knoweth best.

And when we have joined our Helen,
  When we know as we are known,
We will understand it better
  Why He took our lamb so soon.

Of such is the kingdom of God.—Luke 18:16.

Except ye be converted, and become as little children, ye shall not enter the kingdom of Heaven.—Matt. 18:3.

PHILANDER STUMP.

(Written for his Grand-daughter, 1912.)

Philander Stump was my grandpa,
    And he watched me night and day;
For when I was but an infant,
    My own father passed away.

Then I went to live with grandpa,
    That is why I love him so;
And if you had lived with grandpa
    I'm sure you would love him too.

For he was so kind and loving;
    Was so gentle and so good:
And to do one thing to grieve him,
    One would think I never could.

Yet sometimes I'd disobey him;
    Still he knew just what to do,
Though he felt he must deal firmly,
    Yet he dealt so gently too.

How he loved his little Gladys,
   And together they would play
For of her he ne'er grew weary,
   Though she'd follow him all day.

All the neighbors loved my grandpa;
   And the reason you can guess,
For he always went to help them,
   When he found them in distress.

But the reaper Death passed by us,
   Taking my grandpa away,
Although now we cannot see him,
   Still we hope on some bright day,

We will meet him up in Heaven,
   Where together we will sing,
Songs of vict'ry and redemption,
   And of praise unto our king.

So then every one of us shall give an account of
himself to God.—Rom. 14:12.

Part Five.

Miscllaneous Poems or "The Fragments."

He said unto his disciples, "Gather up the fragments that remain that nothing be lost." Therefore they gathered them together and filled twelve baskets with the fragments.—Jno. 6:12, 13.

Twelve Poems.

"INASMUCH."

Inasmuch as ye have done it unto one of the least
of these . . . . ye have done it uno me.—Matt.
25 :40.

Are you wishing that you could go over thhe sea,
   There to sow the good seed of the kingdom of
      God ?
O my friend, just look near you. behold, what
     you see.
For, "The field is the world" saith the Lord, far
     and near,
And if you wish the gospel to give to the lost,
You perhaps will not need to go far from your door.
He who said that repentance and pardon of sins
Should be preached to all nations said also, "Begin
At Jerusalem," meaning at home where they lived.

There are souls whom the Lord will at your hand
     require.
Can you say, with Saint Paul, "I am free from
     their blood"?
Are you sure you have done everything in your
     pow'r,
To convince them of sin, and of One who can save?

Do you teach by example and precept of Christ,
Ever keeping in mind the "Great Day" when He'll
      come,
And shall call for account of each one great and
      small?
Then will you hear the plaudit "Well done" from
      the Lord?
And will He say to you, "Enter into my joy."

Do you know that our Savior is passing each day?
He appears in the form of the naked and cold:
And He often comes hungry, and begging for bread;
He comes oft as a stranger, sometimes as a friend:
He comes now as a wanderer, lost on life's way;
Then He comes seeking guidance and comfort and
      cheer,
He sometimes needs a refuge, a shelter from storm;
He is looking for kindness, He's longing for love.
Are you sure that you know Him each time He
      appears?
Do you always do just as you'll wish you had done?
And when you hear the word, "Inasmuch" from
      the Lord,
"Inasmuch as ye've done" or "did not" will it be?

Inasmuch as ye did it not to one of the least of
these ye did it not to me.—Matt. 25:45.

THE VOYAGE OF LIFE.

When we start upon life's voyage,
    Sailing on the ocean wide,
As we do not know the journey
We should choose a faithful guide:
There'll be storms upon the ocean,
    Angry waves and billows, too,
So we need a strong, brave pilot,
    Who can steer us safely through.

Let's take Jesus for our captain,
    He is strong and brave and true,
He knows every place of danger,
    He will guide us safely through;
With Him we can brave the ocean,
    We can stem the rolling tide,
Till we anchor in the haven,
    Over on the other side.

As we journey with the Master,
    He will give us work to do,
Some of us He may count worthy
To share His suff'ring, too,

If we undertake this voyage
   Without Him who's gone before,
We'll be lost upon the ocean,
   We will never reach the shore.

Let's be loyal to our Captain,
   Trust Him till the journey's o'er,
Till we've gained our home in Heaven,
   Where we meet to part no more..
There'll be shouting and rejoicing,
   When we join that bloodwashed throng,
Jesus' name we'll praise forever,
   As we sing redemption's song.

AN ALLEGORY.

She was weak and faint and weary,
　　She was sad and sick and sore,
She was groping in the darkness—
　　When she saw an open door.

Lo! inside the light was shining,
　　How she longed to enter in,
For her burdens were so heavy,
　　She was seeking rest from sin.

Then she sought to know conditions,
　　And was told, "Turn to the Lord,
And forsake the paths of darkness,
　　Trusting only in His word."

Quickly then she met conditions
　　And as quickly entered in,
Cast on Jesus every burden,
　　Rested from her load of sin.

Then she heard the words of Jesus,
　　Saying, "Let your light so shine

That the sinners out in darkness,
　Passing many at a time,

"May the light see, brightly shining.
　And may pause to hear you tell
Of the path that leads to Heaven
　And the road that leads to hell."

Many souls she helped to rescue
　Out of darkness into light;
Some went bravely to the battle,
　Some to reap where fields were white.

One day, as God's word she pondered,
　Thinking of His wondrous lore,
Suddenly a light flashed on her
　Brighter than she'd seen before.

Long she gazed upon the bright light,
　Then asked, "May I enter too?"
And with rapture heard the answer,
　"This is now God's will for you."

Then with joy she asked conditions,
　Trembled, as she thought them o'er,—
"Give up everything for Jesus,
　Everything you've loved before,

Give up every fond ambition,
  Give up every earthly store,
All that you've held dear or cherished—
  Live for Jesus, nothing more."

Sadly then she slowly answered,
  "No, I cannot pay the price,
Cannot give my all for Jesus,
  Be a living sacrifice."

As she turned away from walking
  In the light God's word has shed,
Everything seemed dark around her—
  Darkness even over head.

So she thought I'll work the harder,
  And I'll shine just as before—
Oil was gone, her lamp was empty,
  In her vessel was no more.

She became alarmed, and questioned,
  As she saw her light grow dim,
Shall I grope again in darkness?
  Or shall I return to Him?

So she turned her eyes to Jesus,
  Saw Him through an open door;

By His side were two oil vessels
  That were filled for ever more.

From each one the oil was carried,
  Through a glistening, golden pipe,
To the lamps, or burning candles,
  That were always clean and bright.

So she cried with deepest anguish,
  Cried to Him with all her might:
"Lord, give me some oil for burning
  So my lamp will shed more light."

Jesus looked on her with pity,
  Longed to hide her in the cleft,
So with loving voice He answered
  "Just come in and help yourself."

If we walk in the light as he is in the light . . .
the blood of Jesus Christ his Son cleanseth us from
all sin.—I John 1:7.

If any man draw back my soul shall have no
pleasure in him.—Heb. 10:30.

OBEDIENCE.

Whatsoever he saith unto you, do it.—Jno. 2 :5.

We should never, never question
　　When the Master bids us go,
Never hesitate nor falter,
　　Never murmur or go slow.

We may know when He is calling,
　　Know what He would have us do,
If we live where He can whisper,
　　"I've a message now for you."

We may always hear from heaven
　　When we pray unto the Lord,
If we keep all His commandments,
　　If we listen to His word.

When two paths come close together—
　　Darkness comes instead of day —
We may always look to Jesus,
　　He is pointing out the way.

If you wish to always prosper
　　In the work you have to do,
Keep the voice of His commandments,
　　Heed the words He says to you.

Would you have whate'er you ask for,
   Do what's pleasing in His sight,
And whatever work He giveth,
   Do it quickly, with thy might.

Jesus, Jesus, blessed Jesus!
   Let us always look to Him,
For His blood so freely flowing
Cleanseth us from all our sin.

Let us love Him, let us praise Him!
   Let us always do His will,
Heeding His command, "Go forward,"
   Pausing when He says, "Stand still."

CHORUS.

Yes, we'll hear the words of Jesus,
   The wonderful, the precious words of Jesus,
Listen to the voice of our Savior,
   Telling what He'd have us do.

If ye love me keep my commandments.—Jno.
14:15.

What thing soever I command you observe to do
it; Thou shalt not add thereto nor diminish from
it.—Deut. 12:32.

A FRIEND IN JESUS.

There is a friend that sticketh closer than a
brother.—Prov. 18:24.

We've found a friend, a friend indeed,
　We've found a friend in Jesus,
And He'll supply our every need;
　We love the name of Jesus.

He's rich in mercy, grace and love
　In Him is hid each treasure:
We only need to look above,
　For blessings without measure.

Since to our hearts the Savior came,
　We wear the Christian armor,
We bravely fight in Jesus' name,
　And give to Him the honor.

While on life's voyage now we sail,
　With Jesus as our Captain,
We're sure to outride every storm,
　And gain the port of heaven.

FIFTY.

Accept this token of our love,
   'Tis sent in fondest memory,
For now your fiftieth year has come,
   Which means the Year of Jubilee.
Yes "fifty" is the best of all,
   For fifty stands for "Pentecost,"
When Jesus sent the Spirit down,—
   "Hast thou received the Holy Ghost?"

Though fifty years have come and gone,
   You need not look for fifty more,
When next the Jubilee, you keep
   'Twill be upon the shining shore;
And as you reach the western slope,
   Which indicates life's setting sun,
"Fear not" for at the journey's end
   You'll hear the Master say, "Well done."

PHILIP.

On the Birth of Philip Edmond LaBounty.

Jno. 1:43-47; 14:6-8; Acts 6:3-5; 8:4-8; 26:35.

O Philip Edmond, we're so glad, so very glad you
came,

For home can never be complete without a baby's
voice.

We read of "Philip" in God's word,—we're glad
you bore his name,

He heard a voice say, "Follow me," and made the
Lord his choice,

He found Nathanael in the way, to him said,
"Come and see."

He came and saw where Jesus dwelt and sought
his righteousness.

When Jesus said, "I am the way, none cometh but
by me,"

Then Philip said, "The Father show, and it
sufficeth us."

And after Christ ascended high and laborers were
few

And they were seeking holy men, with faith and
wisdom tried,

They chose a man named Philip, who was strong
and brave, and true.

But when the church, the church of God, was scat-
     tered far and wide
Then Philip went and preached of Christ to the
     Samaritans.
And in that city there was joy, as words fell from
     his mouth:
And many were the miracles that God wrought by
     his hands,
And then an angel spake to him, "Arise, go toward
     the south."

And as he went, behold, a man was reading in
     God's word.
The Spirit said to Philip, "Go and join thyself
     to him."
The place in Scripture where he read was of the
     Christ our Lord;
Then Philip told how Christ had come and died
     and rose again.
We trust the one who bears this name, will early
     seek the Lord,
And be a soldier of the cross, obeying each com-
     mand,
That God's whole armor he'll put on, and use the
     Holy Sword,
And rich reward receive in Heaven when he has
     gained that land.

FOR THE CHRISTIAN HOME,

AT COUNCIL BLUFFS, IOWA.

God is watching, Brother Lemen,
    Sees your labors day by day;
Listens as you bow in secret,
    Yes, God hears you when you pray.
And no doubt you hear him whisper,
    "Lo, I'm with you all the way."

Great reward awaits in Heaven,
    For the work you're doing now.
Seeds we sow on earth for Jesus,
    He transplants above, somehow.
Here you gather gems to crown Him;
    There they'll shine upon your brow.

You can here afford to suffer
    And a heavy cross to bear,—
E'en go with him to the garden
    Where he struggled long in prayer,—
There to share the Savior's glory,
    And a crown of joy to wear.

O we know our God is working,—
    Working, mightily in you,
Making grace abound and courage
    Filling you with wisdom too.
Only one divinely guided
    Could He trust such work to do.

O this great work for His children!
    You must not bear it alone,
We all want a share in glory
    When Christ cometh for His own.
We can almost hear Him saying
    "Did you help the Christian Home?"

If in heav'n we'd share the glory
    Share the joy your work will bring
We must share in loving service—
    Share with you the suffering,
We must prove our love by giving
    Ere His praises we can sing.

To each member of the Home-band,
    To God's people every where,
We'd say, "Let's help lift this burden,
    Bear it on the wings of prayer.
He who notes the falling sparrow,
    Bids us for His children care.

Dare we rob the God of Heaven,
  By withholding what He gave?
Dare we see His children perish
  And not lift a hand to save?
If so He'll withhold our blessing—
  Every blessing that we crave.

"Call to me and I will answer,
  Great and mighty things I'll show.
I'll instruct and teach and guide thee
  In the way that thou should'st go.
Bring the tithes into my storehouse,
  Prove what blessings I'll bestow."

Yes, He'll give whate'er we ask for,
  If we his commandments keep.—
His commands are, "Love each other."
  "Feed my lambs" and "Feed my sheep"
"Till I come, keep watching, praying;"
  "Weep" He says, "with them that weep."

TO A FRIEND.

(From General Conference.)

O Lola, my dear, we wish you were here
  To help us this feast to enjoy:
We're working each day, yes, toiling away
  Each moment of time we employ.

We're doing our best, we're standing the test,
  We're looking above for the way.
We lean on the Lord, we trust in his word,
  And feel that we're gaining the day.

We're speeding along, we're singing our song,
  We're striving His whole will to do:
Our name we won't tell, you know it too well,
  And that we are thinking of you.

THE CRIMSON STREAM.

The crimson stream will make you free;
　It flows for you, it flows for me.
O, sinner, come and plunge within,
　The blood will wash away your sin.

It was for you that Jesus bled,
　For you His precious blood was shed;
He's pleading now, "Come unto me,"
　O, sinner, listen to the plea.

O, don't refuse, don't turn away;
　He's calling you, He calls today.
O, won't you heed His pleading tone,
　He wants to make you now His own.

CHORUS.

The blood, the blood, that Jesus shed
　　Upon the tree.
The blood, the blood, that Jesus shed
　　On Calvary.
The blood, the blood, that Jesus shed
　　Is all my plea.

The blood of Jesus Christ his Son cleanseth us
from all sin.—1 Jno. 1:7.

OUR SUNDAY SCHOOL.

Come go with us to Sunday school,
　　You'll find a welcome there.
Come old, come young, or rich or poor,
　　For you they'll have a care.

The leader is a man of God,
　　Each teacher knows the Lord;
And ev'ry one attending there
　　Is being taught God's word.

　　Our Sunday school is growing strong,
　　We're sure 'twill gain the day;
And when the Master comes at last
　　"Well done" we'll hear him say.

CHORUS.

Come to our Sunday school,
　　My Sunday school, your Sunday school,
God's Sunday school, we're sure;
　　Come to our Sunday school.

GOD'S BOOKS.

And I saw the dead, small and great, stand before
God; and the books were opened.—Rev. 20:12.

Yes, and sometime the books will be opened;
    Some day the report will be read;
Then we may be surprised at the vision
    For many will rise from the dead,
Wearing crowns filled with stars bright and
    shining,
    Whose names were unknown and unread.

But the lives that we know here and cherish
    Inspire our hearts to be strong:
Their example of trust and devotion,
    In sorrow, temptation, and wrong,
Are all living epistles to show us
    "God leads His dear children along."

He calls some to go forth to the battle,
    While others "remain by the stuff;"
And though sometimes the journey seems tedious
    And often the pathway is rough;
Let's keep working and watching and praying
    Till we hear him say, "'Tis enough."

Part Six.

Children's Department.

Take heed that ye despise not one of these little ones, for I say unto you, That in Heaven their angels do always behold the face of my Father which is in Heaven.—Matt. 18 :10.

PRELUDE.

We would not neglect the children in this little
    book of ours,
For they come to us as blessings, like the dews and
    Summer flowers:
How we love to hear their prattle, love to watch
    them in their play;
And when we are sad or weary, how they cheer us
    on the way!

Yes, there's always room for children, they are use-
    ful ev'rywhere,
And we need their loving service, e'en as they
    need love and care.
Home is not complete without them; without chil-
    dren churches die;
Take them from our state and nation, there would
    be a wailing cry.

Let us nourish then the children, train them as a
    tender vine,—
Their affections are so clinging, how their love our
    hearts entwine.
When we're gone to rest from labor, they'll be
    called to take our place.
By both precept and example, we should fit them
    for the race.

THE KINGDOM.

Unless you come to Jesus
  His little one to be,
The kingdom of the Father
  You'll never, never see.

LITTLE ONES.

I am a very little girl,
  I've only just turned three,
But Jesus loves the little ones,—
  I'm sure that he loves me.

THE STORY.

Mamma still calls me her baby,
  Though I'm almost four years old,
She tells of an infant Savior
  In this Book the story's told.

I'll not tell to you the story,
  You should read it for yourself;
Go home now and get your Bible,
  You will find it on the shelf.

PEARLY GATES.

Unless you seek the Saviour
  "As a little child"—like me,
The "Pearly Gates" of heaven
  You'll never, never see.

THE KINGDOM OF HEAVEN.

Little children were brought
  Unto Jesus one day,
That He might put His hands
  On each one and then pray.

He said, "Suffer the children,"
  To them it is given
"To come, for of such is
  The kingdom of heaven."

A QUESTIONING CHILD.

Last night I said to my papa,
  "May I join the Christian band?"
He said, "Darling, you're too little,
  Wait until you understand.

Must I then be left to perish
  Or to wander from the fold,
Just because I'm weak and little
  And am only six years old?

Jesus said the great and mighty
  Must come "as a little child"
If they'd ever find the Savior,
  Be, like Him, both meek and mild.

Now I'm sure that I love Jesus,
  Know that I can trust him too,
Always run to do his bidding,—
  What more can my papa do?

OUR FATHER'S CARE.

(Three Girls.)

FIRST—THE FLOWERS.

See! the lilies, how they're growing!
    See the grass, and see the trees!
Solomon in all his glory
Was not clothed like one of these.

If the Lord so clothe the flowers ,
    Which are in the field today,
How much more will He clothe children
    Who will follow in the way?

SECOND—THE BIRDS.

God feeds ev'ry coal black raven,
    Notes the sparrows in their fall,
Cares for little worms and insects,—
    He is watching over all.

Why should we His little children,
    Fear to trust Him day by day,
Since we hear Him gently whisper,
    "Ye are better far than they?"

THIRD—THE FLOCKS AND HERDS.

Ev'ry beast in all the forests,
  And the cattle on each hill.
E'en the fowls upon the mountain
God has made to do His will.

Still He loves the little children,
  More than all the flocks and herds
Why should we then fail to trust Him,
  Or, neglect to hear his words?

ALL—THE CHILDREN.

Yes, He clothes us like the lilies,
  And He feeds us like the birds,
And He loves us far more dearly
  Than He loves His flocks and herds.

Father help us all to trust Thee,
  To obey Thy precious word,
Till we're carried by the angels
  To the bosom of our Lord.

OUR CHOICE.

THREE BOYS.

FIRST—SANTA CLAUS.

Now we talk about old Santa,
  As though he were real, and yet,
If he does bring toys and candies,
  Books, and all such things as that,—

He can never give salvation,
  Never could atone for sin.
Santa Claus can't make us holy,
  Clean without and pure within.

SECOND—JESUS.

Jesus Christ, the world's redeemer,
  Is the One who saves from sin.
When we're sorry, he forgives us,
  He can make and keep us clean.

If we only trust in Jesus,
  Do as He would have us do,

In each thought and word and action,
  He will keep us pure and true.

THIRD—THE DIFFERENCE.

Now my friends you see the diff'rence,
  Santa Claus, though rich with toys,
Cannot give to us true riches,
  Cannot save the girls and boys.

If for Santa Claus or Jesus,
  You were called to choose tonight,
Would you for a passing pleasure,
  Lose the joy of heaven's light?

Choose you this day whom ye will serve.—Josh.
24:15.

THE ELECTION.

Let us now have an election,
  Choose our captain for the fight,
For we know the war is raging,
  For the wrong against the right.

Satan stands as one commander,
  Jesus leads His army on.
We must each one fight the battle
  If we'd sing the victor's song.

I for one will vote for Jesus,
  My Commander, He shall be
And I'll be a brave, true soldier,
  Till we gain the victory.

Who, with me, will vote for Jesus?
  Who, for Him, will raise the hand,
Saying "Help me conquer in each conflict.
  Help me for the right to stand"?

He that is not with me is against me, and he
that gathereth not with me scattereth abroad.—
Jesus.

THE NAME OF JESUS.

Have you heard the wondrous story,
　　How to earth an angel came,
Of the message sweet to Mary,
　　When he told the Savior's name?
He said, "Ye shall call him Jesus,
　　For a Savior He shall be:
Blessed art thou, fear not, Mary,
　　For the Lord is now with thee."

CHORUS.

O the blessed name of Jesus,
　　Given long before His birth,
'Tis the sweetest name in heaven,
　　'Tis the sweetest name on earth,
We will praise the name of Jesus,
　　Sing his praises o'er and o'er,
Till we join that happy chorus,
　　Where we'll sing forever more.

Have you heard the wondrous story
   Of the blessed Savior's birth,
When He left His home in heaven
   And came down to live on earth?
How the angels told the shepherds,
   How they went to Bethlehem,
As they heard the angels singing
   "Peace on earth, good will to men?"

Have you heard the wondrous story?
   In a manger He was laid,
For they found no room for Jesus,
   No soft downy bed was made.
Have you heard the wondrous story,
   Of the wise men from afar,
Coming with their richest treasures,
   Guided by a brilliant star?

THE RESURRECTION.

You've often heard the story of the birth of Christ
    the Lord,
When, as a babe he came to earth and took up his
    abode.
Of how he lived and of his death upon Mount
    Calvary,
Where he atonement made for sin to ransom you
    and me.

Now I have came to try to tell a story just as true,
Of Mary and an empty tomb, and of the angels too.
'Twas early in the morning, Mary came with sweet
    perfume
To pour upon the blessed Lord, but found an
    empty tomb.

An angel had been sent from Heaven in raiment
    white as snow,
Who, to the women said, "Fear not, for whom ye
    seek I know."
He rolled away the stone, and then the message
    sweet he told:
"He is not here, the Lord is risen, the place he
    lay behold."

"Go quickly, His disciples tell, He's risen from
the dead."
They ran with fear and trembling now this joyful
news to spread.
And as they went they saw the Lord, they heard
His welcome voice,
Then Jesus took away their fear and made their
hearts rejoice.

If from the dead Christ had not ris'n our faith had
been in vain.
What victory He in triumph wrought when from
the tomb He came,
And in the resurrection morn, when Jesus shall de-
scend,
We'll rise to meet Him and with Him eternal
ages spend.

HOW HE LOVED US.

Jesus left his home in Heaven,
   Jesus left his royal throne,
Came to earth to bring salvation;
   Came for sinners to atone.
Hear him praying in the garden,
   See him hanging on the tree;
See his blood so freely flowing,
   To atone for you and me.

When his arm had wrought salvation,
   When the sacrifice he'd made,
He ascended up to Heaven,
   After ev'ry debt was paid.
There He's building each a mansion
   There He lives to intercede.
We may live with Him in glory,
   Jesus' love is all we need.

CHORUS.

How he loved us, how he loved us;
   How he loves us, loves us still.
He will save us freely, save us,
   If we trust and do His will.

THREE LITTLE GIRLS.

FIRST GIRL.

I wish I had lived in the long time ago,
  When Jesus walked here, on this earth among
      men :
I'm sure I'd have followed wherever He went,
  And He would have blessed me again and again.

SECOND GIRL.

I think it is better to live now, than then,
  For Jesus could then only be in one place :
But now He can watch us wherever we go,
  And feed us, and guide us, and give us His grace.

THIRD GIRL.

Now I think the best time will be up in Heaven,
  Where Jesus has gone to prepare us a place :
For there we can sing with the angels in glory,
  And there we can see our dear Lord face to face.

THE PEARLY GATE.

All—(Singing).

(Air—"Bringing in the Sheaves.")
So we will follow Jesus in our pilgrim journey,
 Until He comes to take us to our home above,
If He shall find us watching, waiting for His com-
  ing,
 So gently He will fold us in His arms of love.
Refrain—
 In His arms of love, in His arms of love,
 So gently He will fold us in His arms of love.
 In His arms of love, in His arms of love,
 So gently He will fold us in His arms of love.

Yes, we will follow Jesus, follow in His footsteps,
 Until He comes to take us we will watch and wait.
Then He will bear us upward, as on wings of eagles
 Till we shall enter heaven through the pearly
  gate.

Refrain—
Through the pearly gate, through the pearly gate,
Till we shall enter heaven through the pearly gate;
Through the pearly gate, through the pearly gate;
Till we shall enter heaven through the pearly gate.

OUR PATTERN.

See, saith he, that thou make all things according to the pattern shewed to thee in the mount.—Heb. 8:5.

One who builds a noble structure,
    Perfect, true in every part,
Always has a perfect pattern
    Which he follows from the start.

So, if we would grow to manhood
    Pure and honest, brave and true,
We should follow in the footsteps
    Of a perfect pattern too.

Jesus is the one to follow,
    By the light of His own word:
We should only follow others
    As they're following the Lord.

Jesus Christ obeyed his parents?
    And revered the Sabbath day;
Always looked above for guidance
    As to what to do and say.

We should follow His example;
　　Do as we know He would do:
Follow also in his precepts,
　　His commands and teachings too.

He would teach us to be humble,
　　Give another the best place,
Not to yield to one temptation,
　　That would hinder in the race.

He was tempted like as we are,
But He always used "the sword:"
Always answered, "It is written,"
Quoting from God's holy word.

When they mocked and spit upon him
He was dumb; he did not speak:
When they asked about his kingdom,
　　In his mouth was no deceit.

O, I long to be like Jesus,
　　In me may His image shine.
I will heed his voice now pleading,
　　"Let me have that heart of thine."

TOBACCO (THREE BOYS.)

FIRST BOY.

My teacher tells me it is wrong,
  For boys to smoke a pipe,
Or smoke cigars or cigarettes;
  She says it is not right.

Now I can't understand this quite,
  In fact I never could,
For my own father smokes each day;
  I'm sure that he is good.

I never heard him swear at all;
  He would not steal I know;
And in those infamous saloons
  I'm sure he does not go.

Now I can't think my father false;
  I know my teacher's true:
When she says this, and he does that,
  Say, what's a boy to do?

SECOND BOY.

I'm glad you ask that question, Bob,
　I'm very glad indeed,
For my pa told me all about
　The vile tobacco weed.

He says that all who learn to use
　The weed in any way,
Soon grow to like it more and more,
　And long for it each day.

In fact, he says they're all made slaves,
　And can't quit if they would;
That often times they see its harm,
　And would stop if they could.

THIRD BOY.

Now boys, I'll tell you what I know;
　I know that Jim is right;
And rather than become a slave,
　I'd go to war and fight.

My father would not tell a lie;
　He always tells the truth.

He smokes and chews this poison weed,
  Has used it from his youth.

I asked him why he did not stop,
  He said, "I can't my son,
My only wish," he said, "Is this
  That I had not begun."

He said, I've now become a slave;
  I'm bound with fetters fast;
I struggle sometimes to be free—
  Am overcome at last.

If to this weed we'd not be slaves
  When we are grown up men,
My father says the secret is,
  We'd better not begin.

THE RESCUE.

Just a word now to those who will own that they're
    slaves,
And who long to be free, but have struggled in
    vain;
For I know there's a ransom, I've found One who
    saves;
    Who can free ev'ry pris'ner, can break ev'ry chain.

For I once was a pris'ner, in bondage to sin,
    To tobacco a slave as one bound by a chain:
How I tried to break loose, tried again and again,
    But I found I was powerless, the triumph to gain.

Then I laid hold on One who was "mighty to save,"
    And am now a man free as a bird of the air,
For I went unto Jesus, a sinner and slave,
    Pleading only His blood, and for mercy and care.

He stooped down, raised me up as to life from the
    dead;
    He unloosed me and let me go perfectly free.
O, I wish you had heard His kind words when He
    said,
    I have loved thee, I've saved thee, come thou fol-
    low me.

O, it pays to serve Jesus, it pays to be true,
  For it brings us a joy that the world cannot give;
And the world cannot take it from me or from you,
  We may always rejoice and triumphantly live.

THE GREATEST GIFT.

We commemorate now the birthday of the One
  Who alone is both able and willing to save;
For when God gave from heaven the gift of his Son
  'Twas the greatest gift earth could receive that
    He gave.

'Tis this Christmas gift, Jesus who'd now make
    you free.
  He would give you the gift of salvation tonight;
If in humble confession you'll now bow the knee,
  He will give you a gleam of eternity's light.

You may rise and go forth as a conquering king,
  For the One who can save, also keeps, day by day;
You may sing songs of vict'ry, in triumph may sing,
  For Jesus has promised to lead all the way.

THE MASTERPIECE.

I stood in the moonlight, I gazed on the stars,
 I went to the forest and looked on the trees,
I saw the great mountains and valleys and hills,
 I watched surging waves on the billowy seas;

I saw the wild beasts and the meek little lambs,
 The birds of the air and the fish of the sea—
It seemed they all echoed the voice of the Lord,
 "If any man thirst let him come unto me."

I found richest treasures hid deep in the earth,
 I saw the ripe fields, and the fruit of the vine,—
They seemed to be saying, 'The earth is the Lord's;
 All kingdom and power and glory are Thine."

The heavens declare all the glory of God;
 The firmament sheweth the works of his hands:
Yet man is the masterpiece God's hand hath
   wrought;
 To man He says, "Love me, obey my commands.'

If forests and mountains and billows and beasts,
 The treasures of earth and the stars of the sky,
The birds of the air and the fish of the sea
 All tell of His glory, should you not, and I?

THE CLOCK.

What says the clock, children, when it strikes one?
"Father in heaven, may thy kingdom come."
What is the answer when striking for two?
"Love one another as I have loved you."
What says the Lord when the clock strikes for three?
"Suffer the children to come unto me."
What's the command when the clock's striking four?
"Joy in our God and rejoice evermore."
What is the message the clock strikes at five?
Ye that are weary God's love will revive."
Hear the clock now, it is striking for six,
When we do wrong 'tis our conscience that pricks.
Now the clock's striking the hour of seven,
"We may inherit the kingdom of heaven."
Each should take warning, the clock's striking eight,
"Enter the kingdom before it's too late."
What's the clock saying? it's striking for nine,
"Thine is the kingdom, the power is Thine."
Hear now the clock, at the hour of ten,
Calling for children again and again.
What is the message it strikes at eleven?
Christ says, "Of such is the kingdom of heaven."
What does the clock say when striking for twelve?
"Those seeking treasures at midnight must delve"

THE DRUNKARD'S SON.

I once knew a boy—the son of a drunkard—
  He hated the life his father had led;
His mother had taught him, wine was a mocker,
  To look not upon it when it was red.
"I'll touch or taste not, e'en look upon it,"
  Again and again, to her he had said.

He grew up from boyhood, strong and so manly,
  For wisdom and lore were first in the quest;
He went to a banquet, gay and so gallant;
  (Knew not that a demon slept in his breast),
Enjoying the feast, the fun and the frolic,
  In each new delight was first and the best.

They then brought the wine, its fumes were ex-
    citing;
  Were all asked to share the finishing toast;
Our youth was surprised, it came unexpected,
  His face was so white,—he looked like a ghost.
He thought, "I can't drink; I won't break my
    promise;"
  Yet feared to offend this hospitable host.

He said, "Please excuse me, I will take water,"
  Then how they all laughed, like he were a knave.
Then whispered a friend, "Take only a little;
  It can't do you harm, be manly and brave;
If you will not drink, 'twill spoil all our pleasure,
  And long you'll regret the trouble you've made."

The host looked upon him sadly and sternly;
  The conflict was great, the enemy strong;
He thought, "Just this once, I'll never more
      touch it,
  For under this pressure, can it be wrong?"
As wine touched his lips, the demon was raging;
  His will-power, strength and manhood were gone.

He quaffed the red wine, drank more and more
      freely;
  Grew gay and talked weird and looked, O, so wild:
His friends were surprised, the host was disgusted,
  While some were alarmed, and some gravely
      smiled.
He lost all his senses and lay there unconscious:
  They said, "Sure enough, the drunkard's own
      child."

www.ingramcontent.com/pod-product-compliance
Lightning Source LLC
Chambersburg PA
CBHW020508040426
42331CB00042BA/99